THE GREAT BOOK OF ANIMAL KNOWLEDGE

FOXES

The Sly Red Creatures

Introduction

Photo by Neil McIntosh (flickr.com/harlequeen), as licensed under CC BY 2.0 Generic

The fox is a well known animal. But did you know that there are 12 species of true foxes, and still some other dog-like animals that can be called foxes? Perhaps the most well known fox is the red fox. The red fox is the largest of the true foxes and it is also the most widespread, they can be found in almost all continents of the world! Let's learn more about the red fox.

What the Red Fox Looks Like

The red fox is a member of the dog family. Red foxes are smaller than wolves and they have pointier snouts than most of the members of the dog family. Red foxes have long legs for running, sharp teeth for tearing meat, long pointed ears that help them hear very well, and a big furry tail.

Size

Photo by jinterwas (flickr.com/jinterwas), as licensed under CC BY 2.0 Generic

Red foxes are about as big as a medium sized dog. They measure 18 to 34 inches from their head to the tip of their tail. Their tail can grow 12 to 22 inches long. Red foxes weigh 12 to 24 pounds (3 to 11 kilograms). Red foxes are usually around 15 inches tall from their feet to the top of their shoulders.

Fur

Red foxes are known for their beautiful fur. Their fur is usually colored red, but sometimes its colored orange or brown. Their coat is often very shiny giving it a nice look when they move around. Red foxes have a white belly, chin, and the tip of their tail is also white. Red foxes were once heavily hunted for their beautiful fur.

Tail

Red foxes are also known for their long, furry tails. The tails of red foxes are so bushy and long that it covers about 30% of their whole body! Red foxes have a patch of white fur on the tip of their tails. The tails of red foxes are used to communicate to each other, to keep them warm, and it helps red foxes balance while they walk, run and jump.

Paws

The paws and legs of red foxes are sometimes colored black. Red foxes have pads on their paws that help them walk easily on almost any terrain. They have sharp claws on their paws that stay out all the time, but can retract a little to their paws so it doesn't get blunt. Red foxes use their claws to fight off predators and hunt for food underground. It is also used for digging dens.

What the Red Fox Eats

Red foxes eat a lot of different things. They usually hunt rodents like squirrels, rabbits, and mice. They also kill and eat birds and lots of different small animals, including insects! Red foxes even eat fruits! In some places, during autumn, red foxes only eat fruits and vegetables. These fruits and vegetables that red foxes eat are several different kinds of berries, apples, grapes, and also acorns. Red foxes also eat garbage, chickens, and other livestock when available.

Senses

Red foxes have great eyesight. It helps them find their way during nighttime. Their sense of smell helps them find dead animals to eat. But the main sense they use for hunting is their sense of hearing. Red foxes have a very strong sense of hearing. They can hear their prey even while it is underground! Red foxes listen very carefully while hunting so they can pinpoint the exact location of their prey.

Hunting

Photo by Russ (flickr.com/russ-w), as licensed under CC BY 2.0 Generic

Red foxes usually hunt during dusk and dawn. They have several hunting techniques. To catch small burrowing rodents they first listen. Once they find the exact location of their prey, the red fox will leap high in the air and land on their prey with incredible accuracy! Red foxes also stalk their prey and chase when they are close. They usually do this when hunting birds and rabbits. Red foxes are also known for two very crafty and unique hunting styles. The first is they will act very playful by themselves to make their prey curious. Once their prey comes close to have a look the red fox will pounce and kill them. The other way is to play dead so birds will land beside them and they can snatch the birds easily.

Hiding Food

Photo by Bart van Dorp (flickr.com/bartvandorp), as licensed under CC BY 2.0 Generic

Red foxes don't have big stomachs. So they can only eat a small amount of food at a time. Red foxes usually store some food underground when there is plenty food so they can eat even when food becomes difficult to find. Red foxes dig a shallow hole, drop their food in, and then cover it up again. They usually have lots of small food stores around their territory.

Where the Red Fox Lives

Red foxes can be found almost everywhere in the northern hemisphere, North America, Asia, Europe and northern Africa. They were also brought to Australia in the 1800s, and they continue to thrive there today. Red foxes can live in almost any type of environment. They can be found in lots of places from hot deserts to snowy mountains!

Territory

Most of the time, red foxes live alone in their own territory. Red foxes will patrol their territory and will leave scent marks so other red foxes know when they are entering someone's territory. Red foxes usually don't enter other territories except if there is little food, when a young male fox leaves his family to look for his own territory, or when finding a mate. Red foxes act differently towards intruders. Usually if a female enters a male's territory, or the other way around, they won't mind each other. But if a stranger of the same gender is found intruding, it usually turns into a fight.

Breeding

Red foxes usually mate during January or February. This is so their baby red foxes will be born during the mild spring weather. Male red foxes are most aggressive when it is almost mating season and there is many fights between them. The winner of the fight has the right to mate with any of the females within his range. Female red foxes usually give birth after 52 days.

Dens

Before a female red fox gives birth, she will prepare one or more dens to give birth in. Sometimes she will dig her own den, but it is more common for her to renovate an abandoned den made by animals like badgers of woodchucks.

Baby Red Foxes

When spring arrives, female red foxes usually give birth to 4 to 6 babies, though sometimes they give birth to as many as 13 babies! Baby red foxes are called kits, cubs, or pups. They are born blind, deaf, and toothless. The mother red fox has to stay with the babies in the den for about two weeks. During this time, the father of the cubs has to bring food to his family. After two weeks, the babies'

eyes open. At about three weeks old they can start to move around. And by the fourth week they start eating food vomited by their parents. The fur of baby red foxes is not colored red. Instead, it is colored grey-brown to help keep them out of sight from predators.

The Life of a Red Fox

Photo by Rylee Isitt (flickr.com/risitt), as licensed under CC BY-SA 2.0 Generic

Baby red foxes start going outside their den at 4 to 5 weeks old. At first, they don't go far from their den. Then as they get older they start exploring more and they start hunting insects. When summer arrives, young red foxes start accompanying their parents to hunts. And at 6 months old, young red foxes are already fully grown. By autumn, young red foxes start spending more time away from their home and will soon leave to find their own territory. Sometimes, young females will not leave their home for a year. These females help their mother raise a new litter of baby red foxes by bringing food. If the mother dies then the helper females will be the ones to raise the young.

Sounds

Photo by Rylee Isitt (flickr.com/risitt), as licensed under CC BY-SA 2.0 Generic

Unlike wolves and coyotes, red foxes don't howl. Instead they have many different sounds to communicate to each other. These sounds include chuckling, whining, whimpering, shrieking, and even shrill screams! Red fox families use these sounds to keep in touch with each other if they get separated, or to warn others of danger. An alarm bark can be heard from about one mile away! The sounds of a red fox have a higher pitch than the sounds of a dog, and can sound like crows or ravens.

Predators

Red foxes have many predators. They have different predators depending on where they are found.   In North America red foxes are hunted by cougars and bobcats. Wolves may also kill and eat red foxes in fights over food. In Europe and Asia, leopards and lynxes prey on red foxes. Red fox remains have also been found in the dens of hyenas. Red foxes can also be killed and eaten by eagles.

Eurasian eagle owls prey on young red foxes while golden eagles may kill even adult red foxes!

Humans and Red Foxes

Photo by Roger Ward (flickr.com/acradenia), as licensed under CC BY 2.0 Generic

Humans have hunted and killed red foxes for a long time. Red foxes are sometimes hunted for their fur. Fox fur can be used for many different types of clothes. When red foxes live near humans, they often kill and eat livestock. So the humans kill the red foxes to protect their livestock. Red foxes are not known to directly attack humans.

True Foxes

There are many types of foxes. But only twelve are classified as vulpes, or true foxes. Red foxes are the only specie of vulpes that can be found in lots of different regions in the world. The other species usually live in just one region. Arctic foxes are found only in northern, cold, arctic places. Bengal, Tibetan sand, Blanford's, and corsac foxes can be found in Asia. Rüppell's foxes can be found in both Asia and Africa. Other foxes in Africa include the cape fox, pale fox, and the smallest of the true foxes, the fennec fox. In North America, you can find kit foxes and swift foxes.

Other Foxes

Despite not being classified as true foxes, there are still some other dog-like animals that may be called foxes. Probably the most well-known one is the gray fox. Gray foxes can be found in the southern half of North America. There are also other kinds foxes found in South America. These are the Andean fox, Darwin's fox, pampas fox, Sechuran fox, hoary fox, and South American gray fox. Crab-eating foxes can also be found in South America.

Get the next book in this series!

CHIMPANZEES: The Smartest Primates on the Planet

Log on to Facebook.com/GazelleCB for more info

Tip: Use the key-phrase "The Great Book of Animal Knowledge" when searching for books in this series.

For more information about our books, discounts and updates, please Like us on Facebook!

Facebook.com/GazelleCB